HO WEAVE WIRE

THE COMPLETE STEP BY STEP BOOK ON WIRE WRAPPING BASICS AND BEYOND

© COPYRIGHT 2024

MICHEAL CAMBEL

Table of Contents

- INTRODUCTION 3
- CHAPTER 1 5
  - ESSENTIAL TOOLS AND MATERIALS 5
- CHAPTER 2 12
  - GETTING STARTED 12
- CHAPTER 3 17
  - BASIC WIRE WEAVING TECHNIQUES 17
- CHAPTER 4 23
  - CREATING SIMPLE PROJECTS 23
- CHAPTER 5 30
  - INTERMEDIATE TECHNIQUES 30
- CHAPTER 6 37
  - ADVANCED WIRE WEAVING TECHNIQUES ... 37
- CHAPTER 7 44
  - PROJECT IDEAS AND TUTORIALS 44
- CHAPTER 8 51
  - FINISHING TOUCHES 51

INTRODUCTION

Wire weaving is a jewelry-making process by which Small wires are connected to create intricate patterns and shapes for jewelry. Rings, bracelets, earrings, pendants, and other types of jewelry can all be made using this method. Wire weaving is prized for its adaptability and capacity for beautiful, precise designs. Wire weaving is suitable for hobbyists and beginners because, unlike traditional metalworking, it does not require soldering or specialized equipment.

History and development

The art of wire weaving dates back thousands of years, as evidenced by the discovery of wire jewelry in the graves of Phoenicians and Egyptians. The wire was twisted and shaped into decorative forms by early artists using simple tools. Wire weaving has developed using methods from many different cultures and eras.

Long ago, Egyptian and Phoenician jewelry, often crafted with gold and silver wire, were early examples of wirework.

During the Medieval Era, European artists developed elaborate wire-wrapped stones and ornamentation as wire-weaving techniques became more widespread.

During the Baroque and Renaissance periods, complex wire-weaving patterns were used to create elaborate jewelry creations.

Wire weaving has become more accessible because of new materials and tools. It is a popular skill among jewelry manufacturers because of its ability to accommodate both classic and contemporary designs.

CHAPTER 1
ESSENTIAL TOOLS AND MATERIALS

Materials and Gauges of Different Types

Gauge refers to the wire's thickness. The greater the check number, the thinner the wire. The following gauges are commonly used in wire weaving.

18-20 gauge is a thicker wire utilized for structural components such as bases and frames.

22-26 Gauge is a Medium-to-fine wire that works well for weaving and wrapping.

28-30 gauge is a very tiny wire used for delicate work and detailed embellishments.

Copper is a cost-effective and commonly utilized material among novices. Because of the numerous coats, it comes in a range of colors and is straightforward to deal with.

Silver Sterling is a popular choice for more expensive jewelry. It lasts a long time and has a beautiful, polished appearance.

Gold-Filled is a very Solid gold that is less expensive but lasts longer than gold plating. A base metal and a thick layer of gold are bound together.

Brass is a less expensive substitute to gold that appears to be identical.

Creative wire is a type of colored copper wire that comes in a range of colors and is frequently enamel-coated.

Pliers, cutters, mandrels, and other basic tools

Pliers:

Chain Nose:

This has Jaws that are tapering in shape, flat on the inside, and rounded on the outside. Ideal for bending and holding wires.

Pliers with Round Nose:

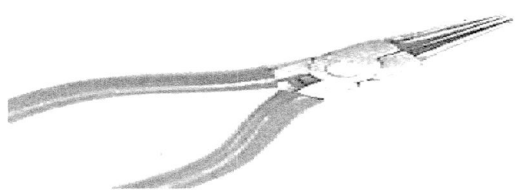

This has Jaws with a tapered, conical shape that is used to form loops and curves in the wire.

Pliers with Flat Nose: it has wide, flat jaws that are useful for securely grasping wire and making exact bends.

Pliers with bent noses:

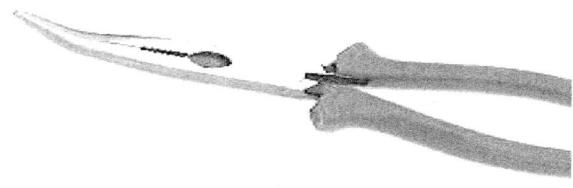

It has angled jaws, which make it simpler to operate in tight spaces and on tiny details.

Cutters

Flush Cutters:

it is used to cut wires flush and cleanly, avoiding sharp edges.

Side Cutters:

This is used to trim extra material and cut thicker wire.

Mandrels

Rings of Mandrel: this is a cylindrical instrument with a taper for shaping and sizing rings.

Mandrel Bracelet: this is a kind of bigger mandrel for making bangles and bracelets.

Additional Essential Tools:

Wire Straightener: used to straighten bent or kinked wire, making it easier to deal with.

Needle files: these are small files used to polish details and smooth rough edges.

Measuring instruments: this includes calipers and a ruler for precise measures.

Accessories for Advanced Techniques

Wire Jig: A device with stakes that permits you to make steady shapes and examples in wire.

Rotary Tool: it is used for polishing, finishing, and drilling holes in metal surfaces.

Tumbling Machine: a tool that uses abrasive materials to rotate wire jewelry to polish and harden it.

Sculpting Hammer: it is a tool used to create decorative effects by adding texture to metal or wire surfaces.

Torch: used to soften wire and make it easier to work with or to solder intricate parts.

Beads and Stones

Gemstones

Semi-precious stones: Color and value are added to your designs by using semi-precious stones like amethyst, turquoise, and garnet.

Cabochons: Smooth, polished stones with no facets that are frequently utilized in wire wrapping.

Glass Beads

Seed beads: Beads of varying sizes are used to create intricate designs and accents.

Beads for Lamp work: Glass beads made by hand in a variety of shapes and colors.

Pearls

Pearls from freshwater: Affordable and available in a variety of sizes and shapes.

Pearls from Culture: higher quality and shaped more uniformly.

Other Beads

Crystal Beads: Make your designs sparkle and look elegant. Crystals from Swarovski are a popular option.

Beads in Wood: Provide a natural, earthy appearance and can be used in mixed media designs with metal.

You can experiment with a wide range of wire weaving techniques and create beautiful, one-of-a-kind jewelry using these tools, materials, and embellishments.

CHAPTER 2
GETTING STARTED

Best Practices and Safety Tips

Safety Advice

Protect Your Hands: Always put on finger protectors or gloves to avoid being cut or burnt by the wire. Also To reduce strain, make use of forceps with comfortable handles.

Safety of Eye: it is important to Wear a safety glass at all times to protect your eyes from flying wire or beads.

Ventilation: working in a well-ventilated environment is vital especially when using a torch, chemicals, or adhesives.

Tool upkeep: always keep your tools in good working order. In comparison to dull tools, sharper ones are safer and more effective.

Appropriate positioning: Choose a chair that is comfortable for you and work at a table height that doesn't force you to bend over to prevent stressing your neck and back.

Keep Your Workspace Neat: A well-organized workspace minimizes accidents and makes it easier to locate equipment and supplies.

Tips for Organizing Your Design: To make sure you have a clear plan, start by sketching your designs.

Cut Once, Measure Twice: To prevent waste, always double-check your dimensions before cutting the wire.

Proceed slowly and with caution: To be precise and prevent errors, take your time.

Methods of Practice: Use leftover wire to practice different weaving techniques before starting a project.

Maintain Orderliness: Arrange your equipment and materials so they are simple to locate and utilize.

Selecting an Ideal Site for Your Office: You need good light for detailed work. So make sure to use a desk lamp with a magnifying lens if needed.

Durable Surface for Work: Use a desk or table that is large enough to accommodate your tools and supplies.

Methods for retaining: Organize your tools, wires, and beads using trays, drawers, or other containers to help keep them neat. To make storage containers easier to locate, label them.

Comfortable seating: Choose a chair that can be adjusted and promotes proper posture.

Tool accessibility: Tools that you use often should be kept handy to help you fasten your productivity.

Safety equipment: Have safety glasses, a first aid kit, and gloves handy.

Understanding Wire Gauge Hardness

Wire Gauges System: Wire gauges are measured using the American Wire Gauge (AWG) system. The wire gets thinner with increasing check number.

Sample Meters:

18-20 Gauge: The thicker wire is commonly used for structural components such as frames.

22-26 gauge: Medium to fine wire used for weaving and wrapping.

28-30 gauge: Extremely fine wire, is often used for beautiful detailing.

The wire's hardness

Dead soft: Easily formed and incredibly flexible. Perfect for complex weaving and wrapping, but not as durable.

Half-Hard: a harmony of suppleness and strength. Ideal for creating objects that require the preservation of their structural components and form.

Full-Hard: exceedingly rigid and hard. Ideal for extremely durable components such as structural frames and clasps.

How to Pick the Correct Wire Project Requirements: Examine the objectives and design of the project. Use thicker wire for delicate weaving and structural features.

Benefits of the Materials: distinct metals have distinct qualities. In contrast, copper is less flexible than silver, and wire that has been filled with gold is also more flexible.

Aesthetics: Select wire that complements your beads and stones. Wires that are coated and colored can add a distinctive visual aspect to your designs.

If you understand how to make use of tools, determine which types of wire to use, and organize your workspace, you will be able to create beautiful and skillfully made wire-woven jewelry.

CHAPTER 3

BASIC WIRE WEAVING TECHNIQUES

Single Weave

Portrayal: The single weave is the simplest type of wire weaving, where a thin wire is woven around a thicker base wire to make a clear pattern.

Steps:

Secure the Wires: Begin by anchoring the thin weaving wire around the base wire with a couple of tight loops.

Weave: Pass the weaving wire and under the base wire in a persistent movement, keeping up with even spacing.

Proceed: Keep the pressure steady and weave until you arrive at the ideal length.

Finish: Secure the end by wrapping the weaving wire firmly around the base wire a couple of times and trim any overabundance.

Applications: This technique is frequently utilized for simple rings and armbands and as a primary strategy in additional complex designs.

Double Weave

Depiction: The double weave includes weaving a slim wire over and under two base wires, creating a more intricate and solid example.

Steps:

Secure the Wires: Anchor the weaving wire around one of the base wires.

Weave: Pass the weaving wire the respectable starting point wire, under the second, and afterward back throughout the second and under the first. This makes a double circle around each wire.

Proceed: Keep up with even pressure and dividing as you weave this way and that.

Finish: Secure the end by wrapping the weaving wire around one of the base wires a few times and trim any overabundance.

Applications: This procedure is valuable for making more grounded and more definite jewelry pieces like sleeves and elaborate pendants.

Figure 8 Weave

Depiction: The Figure 8 weave includes creating a consistent figure-eight example around at least two base wires.

Steps:

Secure the Wires: Anchor the weaving wire around one of the base wires.

Weave: Pass the weaving wire at the highest point of the respectable starting point wire, around it, then, at that point, over the respectable halfway point wire and around it, shaping a figure-eight pattern.

Proceed: Rehash this interaction, keeping the pressure and dispersing predictable.

Finish: Secure the end by wrapping the weaving wire around one of the base wires a few times and trim any overabundance.

Applications: This weave adds an ornamental touch to rings, wristbands, and pendants, and can be utilized to make intricate designs.

Basket Weave

Portrayal: The basket weave includes weaving a meager wire around multiple base wires in a pattern that looks like a woven basket.

Steps:

Secure the Wires: Anchor the weaving wire around one of the base wires.

Weave: Pass the weaving wire and under multiple base wires in a volatile movement, creating a woven pattern.

Proceed: Keep up with dividing and strain as you weave the example.

Finish: Secure the end by wrapping the weaving wire around one of the base wires a few times and trim any overabundance.

Applications: This procedure is great for creating wide armbands, pendants, and intricate designs that require a finished look.

Coiling Techniques

Depiction: Coiling includes wrapping a thin wire firmly around a base wire to make a winding pattern.

Steps:

Secure the Wires: Anchor the thin wire around the base wire with a couple of tight curls.

Coil: Wrap the slim wire firmly around the base wire in a ceaseless winding, keeping the loops near one another.

Proceed: Keep up with even strain and divide as you loop the wire.

Finish: Secure the end by folding the snaked wire over the base wire a few times and trim any overabundance.

Varieties:

Single Coil: One layer of curls around the base wire.

Double Coil: Two layers of curls, one over the other, for added thickness and surface.

Coiled Beads: Adding beads at stretches to the coiling wire for an improved impact.

Applications: Coiling is utilized to add embellishing components, reinforce designs, and make central focuses in jewelry pieces.

These basic wire-weaving techniques structure the establishment for additional complex designs and are essential abilities for any wire-weaving jewelry producer.

CHAPTER 4
CREATING SIMPLE PROJECTS

Creating Simple Projects

Making a Basic Wire Wrapped Ring

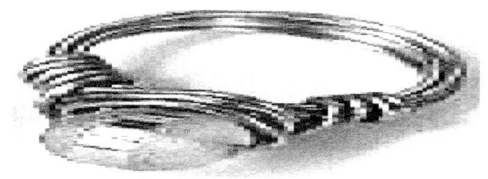

Materials and Tools:

18-20 gauge wire for the base

26-28 gauge wire for wrapping

A mandrel or ring-estimating instrument

Wire cutters

Round nose pliers

Chain nose pliers

A bead or little gemstone (optional)

Steps:

Cut the Base Wire: Cut a length of 18-20 gauge wire, around 8-10 inches long, contingent upon the ideal ring size and plan.

From the Ring Base:

Fold the base wire over the mandrel at the ideal ring size. Leave equivalent lengths of wire on one or the other side of the ring.

Get the wires close to one another to get the shape.

Add a Bead (Optional):

Slide a bead or little gemstone onto one of the wire closes.

Position the bead at the focal point of the ring's top.

Wrap the Wires:

Utilizing the round nose pliers, make a little circle close to the foundation of the bead (if utilizing).

Wrap the wire close around the ring base to get the bead set up. Keep wrapping firmly to make a flawless and brightening design.

Finish the Ring:

Trim any overabundance of wire utilizing the wire cutters.

Fold the wire closes conveniently utilizing affix nose pliers to stay away from sharp edges.

Smooth and change the ring on the mandrel for the last shape.

Clean:

Tenderly clean the ring to eliminate any device checks and give it a completed look.

Crafting Simple Earrings

Materials and Tools:

20-22 gauge wire for the earring base

26-28 gauge wire for wrapping

Beads or little gemstones

Earring hooks

Wire cutters

Round nose pliers

Chain nose pliers

Steps:

Cut the Base Wire: Cut two equivalent lengths of 20-22 gauge wire, around 3-4 inches each, for the earring bases.

Make the Earring Casing:

Utilizing round nose pliers, structure a little circle toward one side of each wire.

Shape the wire into a tear or wanted shape, passing on a little tail at the top to join the earring hook.

Add Beads: Slide beads or gemstones onto the base wire, situating them in the middle or along the edge as wanted.

Wrap the Wire:

Utilizing the 26-28 gauge wire, begin wrapping from the circle at the top, securing the beads set up.

Wrap firmly and uniformly, adding enriching loops as wanted.

Append Earring Hooks:

Utilize the chain nose pliers to open the circle at the lower part of the earring hook.

Append the earring casing to the hook and close the circle safely.

Finish the Earrings:

Trim any abundance wire and fold the closures flawlessly.

Rehash the interaction for the subsequent earring.

Designing a Basic Wire Wrapped Pendant

.

Materials and Tools:

18-20 gauge wire for the pendant base

26-28 gauge wire for wrapping

A central bead or cabochon

Wire cutters

Round nose pliers

Chain nose pliers

Flat nose pliers

Steps:

Cut the Base Wire: Cut a length of 18-20 gauge wire, around 10-12 inches, contingent upon the size of the pendant.

Structure the Pendant Casing:

Utilizing round nose pliers, make a circle toward one side of the wire for the pendant bail.

Shape the wire into an edge to fit the central bead or cabochon, passing on sufficient wire toward the finish to get the bead.

Secure the Central Bead:

Place the bead or cabochon at the focal point of the casing.

Utilizing the leftover wire, wrap firmly around the bead to hold it set up. Make brightening twirls or loops as wanted.

Add Brightening Wraps:

Utilizing the 26-28 gauge wire, fold over the casing and bead to add security and embellishing components.

Make intricate patterns or simple curls, contingent upon your plan inclination.

Finish the Pendant:

Trim any abundance wire and fold the closures conveniently.

Change the pendant shape with level nose pliers if necessary.

Clean:

Tenderly clean the pendant to eliminate any instrument stamps and give it a complete look.

These simple projects assist novices with rehearsing basic wire weaving and wrapping techniques while creating wonderful, wearable gem pieces.

CHAPTER 5
INTERMEDIATE TECHNIQUES

Intermediate Techniques

Adding Beads and Stones

Adding beads and stones to wire weaving projects can improve their excellence and complexity. Here are a few basic techniques:

Basic Wire Wrapping with Beads:

Stage 1: Cut a length of wire (20-24 gauge).

Stage 2: Slide the bead onto the wire, situating it in the center.

Stage 3: Overlay the wire around the bead, then, at that point, curve the wires together over the bead to get it.

Stage 4: Use round nose pliers to make a little circle over the bead, folding the wire over the circle's base a few times to get it. Trim any overabundance of wire.

Incorporating Beads into Weaves:

Figure 8 Weave: Slide a bead onto one of the base wires before moving over to the following wire. This method puts the bead inside the weave.

Basket Weave: Add beads at spans, putting them on the base wires as you weave the flimsy wire over and under.

Wrapping Cabochons:

Stage 1: Cut two pieces of wire (20-24 gauge) adequately long to fold over the cabochon with extra for the bail.

Stage 2: Structure a casing around the cabochon with the wires, crossing them at the top.

Stage 3: Utilize a more slender wire (26-28 gauge) to fold over the casing, securing the cabochon setup.

Stage 4: Make a bail with the wire closures and get done with brightening wraps or curls.

Combining Weaves

Combining different weaving techniques in a single project can make more intricate and outwardly fascinating designs.

Double and Figure 8 Weave Blend:

Begin with a double weave for the base.

Progress into a Figure 8 weave to add surface and complexity.

Single Weave and Basket Weave Blend:

Start with a single weave around a base wire.

Consolidate a basket weave in segments to add aspect and variety.

Blending Wire Gauges:

Utilize thicker wire for the primary base and more slender wire for intricate weaves.

Join various gauges inside a single project to make fluctuating surfaces and qualities.

Model Project: Complex Pendant:

Stage 1: Make a casing with thicker wire (18-20 measure) in a tear shape.

Stage 2: Begin with a single weave around the casing.

Stage 3: Change to a double weave in the center segment.

Stage 4: Add beads or stones utilizing a Figure 8 weave.

Stage 5: Get done with brightening basket weaves on the lower part of the pendant.

Creating Clasps and Connectors

Making your clasps and connectors can add a customized touch to your gems and guarantee they match your plan impeccably.

Simple Hook and Eye Clasp:

Hook:

Stage 1: Cut a piece of wire (18-20 gauge) around 3-4 inches long.

Stage 2: Utilizing round nose pliers, make a little circle toward one side.

Stage 3: Twist the wire into a snare shape.

Stage 4: Make another little circle or curl the wire end to get the snare.

Eye:

Stage 1: Cut a piece of wire around 2 inches long.

Stage 2: Make a little circle toward one side utilizing round nose pliers.

Stage 3: Curve the wire back on itself to frame a figure 8 shape.

S-Clasp:

Stage 1: Cut a piece of wire (18-20 check) around 4 inches long.

Stage 2: Utilizing round nose pliers, make a circle toward one side of the wire.

Stage 3: Curve the wire into an "S" shape.

Stage 4: Make one more circle at the opposite end, ensuring the two circles are looking inverse bearings.

Wire Wrapped Circle Connector:

Stage 1: Cut a piece of wire (20-24 measure) around 2-3 inches long.

Stage 2: Utilizing round nose pliers, structure a circle toward one side.

Stage 3: Fold the tail of the wire over the foundation of the circle a few times to get it.

Stage 4: Make one more circle at the opposite end and secure it with wraps.

Stage 5: Trim any overabundance of wire and wrap up the closures with chain nose pliers.

Beaded Connector:

Stage 1: Cut a piece of wire (20-24 measure) around 3 inches long.

Stage 2: Slide a dab onto the wire, centering it.

Stage 3: Make a circle toward one side utilizing round nose pliers and fold the wire over the foundation of the circle to get it.

Stage 4: Rehash on the opposite finish to make a beaded connector with circles on the two closures.

By mastering these techniques, you can make intricate and lovely wire-wrapped gems that integrate beads, join various weaves, and incorporate custom clasps and connectors for expert completion.

CHAPTER 6
ADVANCED WIRE WEAVING TECHNIQUES

Advanced Techniques

Complex Patterns and Designs

Making complex patterns and designs in wire weaving includes joining different weaving techniques and adding mind-boggling details.

Layered Weaves:

Join various weaves (e.g., basket weave, figure 8) in layers to make a finished, multi-layered look.

Model: Begin with a basket weave base, add a layer of Figure 8 weave, and wrap up with single weave details.

Balanced Designs:

Make adjusted designs by reflecting weaves and patterns on one or the other side of a focal point of convergence, similar to a gemstone or cabochon.

Model: Even pendants with a focal stone and reflected wire patterns on each side.

Mind-boggling Patterns:

Utilize fine check wire (28-30) to make sensitive, ribbon-like patterns.

Model: Plan a pendant with a perplexing filigree design utilizing fine wire to make circles and whirls.

Enhancing Components:

Add little enriching components like twisting's, loops, and bead bunches to improve the plan.

Model: Make a wire-wrapped wristband with little winding accents and bead groups along the band.

Working with Different Wires

Working with different wires takes into account more complex designs and more grounded structures.

Parallel Weaving:

Utilize different base wires next to each other, weaving around them to make wide, level designs.

Model: A wide-sleeve wristband with four parallel base wires woven along with a figure 8 weave.

Braid Weave:

Braid at least three wires together, consolidating globules and stones as you go.

Model: A braided jewelry with beads woven into the braid for added surface and variety.

Stacked Weaves:

Stack various weaves on top of one another for a layered impact.

Model: A pendant with a base layer of single weave, a center layer of twofold weave, and a top layer of complicated figure 8 weave.

Wire Edges:

Make solid wireframes with different wires for huge, organized designs.

Model: A wireframe for a huge cabochon, wrapped with various wires to get and embellish the stone.

Consolidating Mixed Media

Consolidating mixed media can add remarkable surfaces and varieties to your wire-weaving projects.

Fabric and Ribbon:

Weave fabric or ribbon into wire designs for added variety and surface.

Model: A wristband with wire weaving scattered with segments of brilliant ribbon.

Leather and Cord:

Join leather or cord with wire weaving for a provincial or bohemian look.

Model: A pendant with a leather cord base, decorated with wire weaving and beads.

Resin and Polymer Clay:

Use resin or polymer clay components inside your wire designs.

Model: A wire-wrapped pendant with a polymer clay highlight or resin cabochon.

Tracked down Articles:

Integrate found objects like shells, quills, and stones into your wire weaving.

Model: A neckband highlighting a wire-wrapped shell or quill as the point of convergence.

Mixed Metals:

Join various metals (e.g., copper, silver, gold-filled) for differentiating tones and wraps up.

Model: A couple of hoops with exchanging segments of copper and silver wire weaving.

Model Task: Mixed Media Explanation Accessory

Materials:

Numerous wires in various measures (18-28) and metals (copper, silver).

Beads, stones, and a focal cabochon.

Ribbon or leather cord.

Polymer clay or resin components (discretionary).

Fundamental devices: pliers, cutters, mandrel.

Steps:

Stage 1: Make a wireframe for the focal cabochon utilizing an 18-check wire. Secure the cabochon with a twofold weave.

Stage 2: Add globules and stones to the edge utilizing a figure 8 weave with 26-check wire.

Stage 3: Integrate ribbon or leather cord into the sides of the accessory by weaving it with wire.

Stage 4: Add embellishing components like twisting's, curls, and little polymer clay or resin pieces.

Stage 5: Get done with a catch made from a similar wire, guaranteeing it matches the general plan.

By dominating these advanced techniques, you can make complex, lovely, and one-of-a-kind wire-wrapped gem pieces that grandstand your expertise and inventiveness.

CHAPTER 7

PROJECT IDEAS AND TUTORIALS

Intermediate Ring Projects

Multi-Stone Ring:

Materials:

18-20 gauge wire for the base

26-28 gauge wire for wrapping

Little gemstones or beads

Ring mandrel

Wire cutters, round nose pliers, chain nose pliers

Steps:

Base Frame: Cut a piece of 18-20 gauge wire to the point of folding over the mandrel multiple times.

Wrap and Secure: Structure the base by folding the wire over the mandrel. Leave equivalent lengths of wire on one or the other side.

Add Stones: Position little gemstones or beads on the top wire. Secure them by wrapping the 26-28 gauge wire around each globule and base wire.

Improving Curls: Add enhancing loops on the sides by enveloping the more slender wire with a twisting example.

Finish: Secure the closures of the wire by tucking them perfectly and smooth any unpleasant edges.

Woven Band Ring:

Materials:

20 gauge wire for the base

28 gauge wire for winding around

Ring mandrel

Wire cutters, round nose pliers, chain nose pliers

Steps:

Cut Base Wires: Cut two bits of 20 gauge wire, each lengthy enough to fold over the mandrel with some extra for securing.

Anchor Winding around Wire: Begin winding with the 28 gauge wire by securing it around one of the base wires.

Winding around: Utilize a figure 8 wind to join the two base wires, making a woven band.

Change and Shape: Change the winding on the mandrel to guarantee the right ring size.

Secure Finishes: Wrap up any remaining details and trim the excess wire.

Complex Earrings Designs

Light fixture Earrings:

Materials:

20 gauge wire for the base frame

28 gauge wire for winding around

Little beads or crystals

Earring hooks

Wire cutters, round nose pliers, chain nose pliers

Steps:

Make Frame: Structure a tear or round frame with the 20 gauge wire.

Add Beads: String little beads onto the 28 gauge wire and fold them over the frame.

Winding around: Utilize a figure 8 or container wind to get the beads and add enriching patterns.

Hangs: Make little bead hangs with headpins and join them to the lower part of the frame.

Append Hooks: Associate the frame to the earring hooks with little circles.

Filigree Drop Earrings:

Materials:

22-24 gauge wire for the base

28-30 gauge wire for winding around

Little beads or gemstones

Earring hooks

Wire cutters, round nose pliers, chain nose pliers

Steps:

Make Drop Shape: Structure a drop shape with the 22-24 gauge wire.

Filigree Patterns: Make intricate filigree patterns inside the drop shape with the 28-30 gauge wire.

Add Beads: Integrate little beads or gemstones inside the filigree design.

Finish Closures: Secure the closures of the wire and connect earring hooks.

Intricate Pendant and Necklace Projects

Wire-Wrapped Cabochon Pendant:

Materials:

18-20 gauge wire for the frame

26-28 gauge wire for wrapping

Cabochon stone

Chain or string for a necklace

Wire cutters, round nose pliers, chain nose pliers

Steps:

Make Frame: Cut a piece of 18-20 gauge wire to the point of shaping a frame around the cabochon.

Secure Cabochon: Fold the wire over the cabochon to make a solid frame. Cross the wires at the top to shape the bail.

Improving Wraps: Utilize the 26-28 gauge wire to fold over the frame and add enhancing components.

Make Bail: Structure a bail at the top by bending the wires close together and circling them.

Finish: Secure the closures and join the pendant to a chain or string.

Multi-Strand Beaded Necklace:

Materials:

20-22 gauge wire for connectors

Beads or gemstones

Chain or rope

Wire cutters, round nose pliers, chain nose pliers

Steps:

Make Beaded Strands: String beads onto the wire or beading string to make different strands of shifting lengths.

Interface Strands: Utilize little circles or connectors to join the strands to a focal wire frame.

Make Point of convergence: Design a central pendant or component to connect at the focal point of the multi-strand necklace.

Join Fasten: Secure the closures of the wire strands and connect a catch to the finishes of the necklace.

By handling these intermediate projects, you can expand upon your primary abilities and make more refined wire-wrapped adornments.

CHAPTER 8

FINISHING TOUCHES

Polishing and Finishing Techniques

Authentic polishing and finishing can overhaul the appearance and strength of your wire-wrapped jewelry.

Fundamental Polishing:

Materials: Polishing textures, microfiber textures.

Steps:

Clean: Wipe your piece with a saturated texture to take out any waste or oils.

Clean: Use a polishing texture to buff the wire, applying fragile strain to bring out the radiance.

Last Wipe: Use a microfiber texture to give it a last wipe for a mind blowing culmination.

Tumbling:

Materials: Rotational tumbler, solidified steel shot, water, dish chemical.

Steps:

Load the Tumbler: Spot your jewelry and treated steel shot into the tumbler barrel.

Add Water and cleaning agent: Burden up with adequate water to cover the things and add an unobtrusive amount of dish cleaning agent.

Run the Tumbler: Close the barrel securely and run the tumbler for 2-4 hours.

Wash and Dry: Kill the jewelry, flush it totally, and dry it with a fragile texture.

Hand Polishing with Instruments:

Materials: Dremel instrument with polishing associations, polishing compound.

Steps:

Apply Compound: Apply a humble amount of polishing compound to the association.

Clean: Carefully run the instrument over the wire, ensuring even incorporation and avoiding excessive strain.

Buff: Use an ideal association with buff the piece of a high shimmer.

Adding Patinas: Patinas can add a collectible or innovative concentration to your wire-wrapped jewelry.

Liver of Sulfur Patina:

Materials: Liver of sulfur gel or protuberances, high-temperature water, plastic or glass compartment, baking pop, water.

Steps:

Plan Course of action: Separate a restricted amount of liver of sulfur in steaming hot water.

Plunge Jewelry: Lower the jewelry in the course of action until the ideal tone is achieved.

Kill: Take out the piece and dive it into a baking pop and water answering to kill the patina.

Flush and Dry: Wash totally with water and dry with a sensitive texture.

Antacid and Salt Patina:

Materials: Antacid, salt, plastic holder, wire rack.

Steps:

Set Up: Spot a wire rack in a plastic holder and sprinkle salt over the rack.

Apply Smelling salts: Put the jewelry on the rack and add antacid to the lower part of the holder without reaching the jewelry.

Close and Delay: Close the holder and leave it present moment to cultivate the patina.

Flush and Dry: Wash the jewelry with water and dry it with a sensitive material.

Vinegar and Salt Patina:

Materials: Vinegar, salt, plastic holder.

Steps:

Mix Plan: Mix vinegar and salt in a holder.

Lower Jewelry: Spot the jewelry in the game plan and permit it to sit for a couple of hours.

Flush and Dry: Wash totally with water and dry with a fragile material.

Securing and Strengthening Your Pieces

Ensuring your jewelry is secure and intense is central for quality and life expectancy.

Authentic Wrapping:

Tight Wraps: Assurance all wraps are tight and secure. Free wraps can cripple the development.

For sure, even Pressure: Apply even strain while wrapping to stay aware of consistency and strength.

Developing Affiliations:

Extra Wraps: Add extra wraps at affiliation centers for added strength.

Twist around: Use two pieces of wire for key hidden parts to overhaul strength.

Securing Completions:

Overlap Completions: Crease all wire closes impeccably to prevent getting and increase security.

Trim Excess: Trim any excess wire close to the base and use pliers to smooth and get the completions.

Adding Glue: E6000 Glue: Use an unassuming amount of E6000 stick on fundamental affiliation centers to add extra security.

Application: Apply sparingly with a toothpick and grant it to dry.

Strengthening Shaky parts:s

Secure Beads: fixed beads and stones are securely wrapped and can't move inside their settings.

By merging these polishing, patina, and securing techniques, you can redesign the greatness, strength, and noteworthy ability of your wire-wrapped jewelry.

Printed in Dunstable, United Kingdom